DIESELS
on the
EASTERN

Cambridge
37102

DIESELS on the EASTERN

John Vaughan

LONDON

IAN ALLAN LTD

First published 1983

ISBN 0 7110 1270 9

Published by Ian Allan Ltd, Shepperton, Surrey;
and printed by Ian Allan Printing Ltd at their works
at Coombelands in Runnymede, England

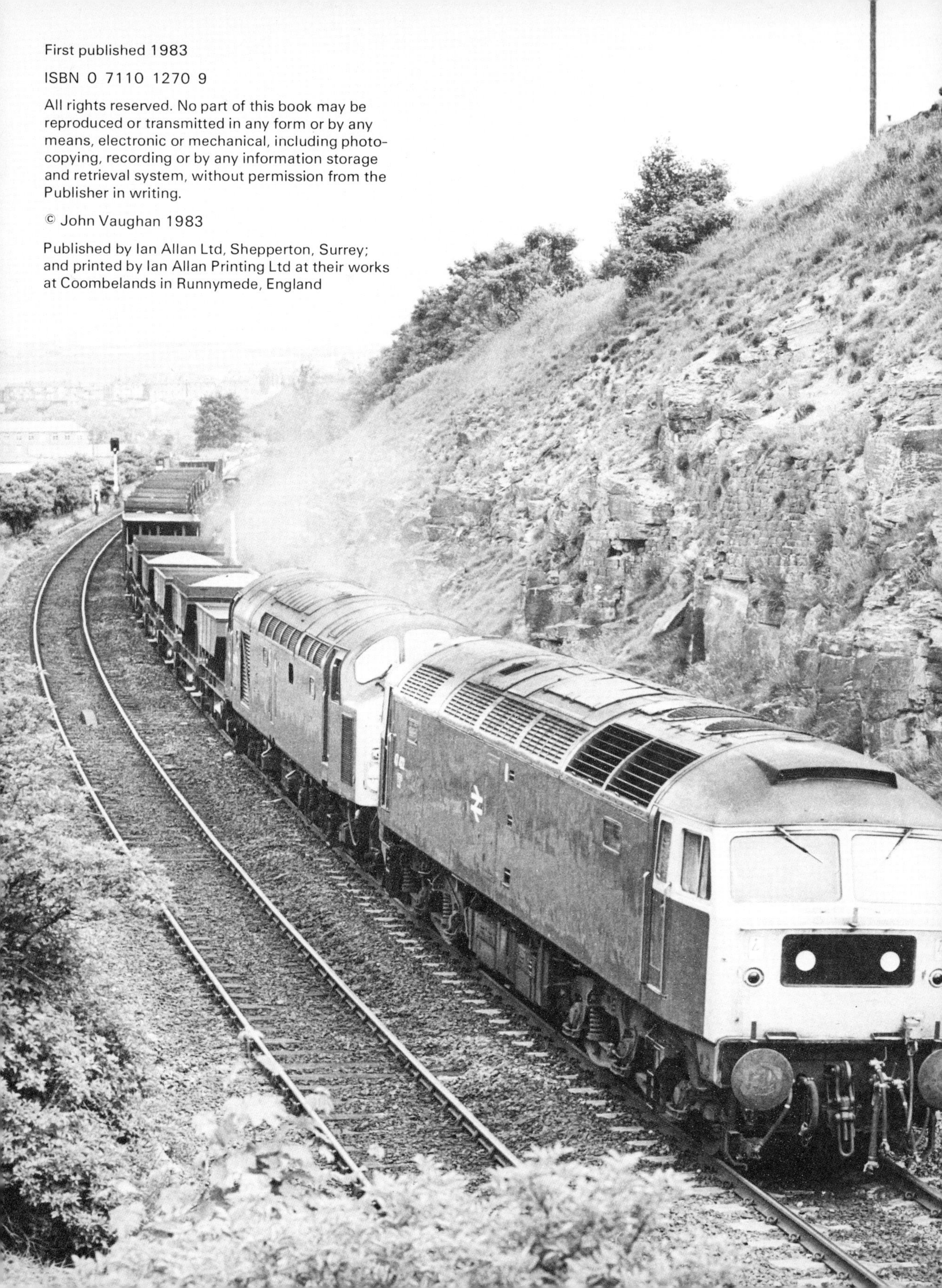

Contents

Front cover: On the ECML the main port of call to the north of Doncaster is Selby. There is a famous swing bridge north of the station over the River Ouse. The whole of this complex will be by-passed by a new route from a point called Colton Junction to Temple Hirst Junction. One can almost hear this Class 40 'opening the taps' with an up freight on 12 April 1980. No 40.010 (formerly *Empress of Canada* and now withdrawn) was recovering from the speed restriction over the bridge. *John Oxley*

Back cover: Full chat at Thornhill. Class 56s are normally associated with the modern air braked freights, especially mgr trains, but on 13 September 1981 No 56.022 strayed on to more mundane duties. Opening-up its Ruston-Paxman engine No 56.022 shows a trail of exhaust and keeps this line of empty coal wagons on the move. *Gavin Morrison*

Title page: No 37.102 in the snow at Cambridge on 12 December 1981 with train 1L45, the 09.52 Cambridge-Liverpool Street. The driver re-enters his cab after attending to the steam pipe between the locomotive and the first coach. By the mid-1980s Cambridge traffic will be exclusively in the hands of ubiquitous emus and overhead wires will clutter this view. *Barry J. Nicolle*

This page: A very interesting combination of motive power at Dewsbury. The train is a typical Sunday engineers special conveying track ballast to the site of pw workings. No 47.422 double heads No 40.035 on 17 June 1979. The locomotives are not compatible for multiple working and hence they will be operating in tandem with a crew in each machine. *Gavin Morrison*

Introduction

The introduction of diesel traction on the Eastern Region started in earnest in 1956 when diesel multiple-units were introduced in East Anglia. Until the mid-1950s the ER had an allocation of diesel shunters but the widespread use of early prototype main line diesels was restricted to Southern and London Midland Region lines and to a lesser extent the Western Region. East Anglia and Lincolnshire had an extensive network of rural branch lines and the introduction of dmus was to benefit these areas by replacing aged steam locomotives and rolling stock and to effect economies in operation. In fact the GER lines of East Anglia had a full dmu scheme implemented by 1959. The prototype 'Deltic' operated on the ER in the late 1950s but it was the introduction of the Mirrlees engined Brush Type 2, later to become known as Class 31, which heralded the arrival of series production diesels, when it was delivered to Stratford depot in October 1957. This was followed by the first of the 2,000hp English Electric Type 4s or Class 40s in the early part of 1958. The first 10 Class 40s were allocated to Stratford and Hornsey depots and by April the new diesels were employed on main line express trains. By June 1958 even the famous 'Flying Scotsman' was frequently diesel hauled.

One of the early problems of the diesel-electric locomotives of the era was their very poor power-to-weight ratio and 138-ton locomotives produced a maximum of 2,000hp which resulted in a performance which was no better than a 'Pacific' steam locomotive. This situation was to change dramatically with the arrival of the 'Deltic' Class 55 locomotives but the operators had to wait until 1961 for these 3,300hp 100ton machines. In the meantime most of the diesel 'action' was in the London area and the dieselisation story of the late 1950s was a far from happy one. In the latter part of 1958 the small 800hp Paxman engined North British Type 1s or Class 16s were introduced, followed by the 1,100hp Class 29s and the 1,100hp Class 23 'Baby Deltics'. In terms of availability all three classes were an operational disaster and unfortunately the ER lost considerable creditability as failure followed failure. Fortunately new classes of diesel locomotives in the middle power range were being introduced simultaneously and in the 1958/9 period more Class 31s and the small Sulzer engined Class 24s were introduced. These joined forces with a batch of 20 Birmingham R. C. W. Sulzer engined Class 26s to keep the GN suburban services in operation. On the freight side the first Class 20s had arrived in the London area and although initially allocated to Devons Road, Bow, the class found themselves on passenger trains during the early 1960s, despite their lack of train heating facilities, when the whole 'Baby Deltic' fleet was banned from passenger work.

The British Thomson-Houston 800hp Class 15s were also active but as with the Class 16s they were underpowered. Although the Class 26 and 29 locomotives were to be transferred to Scotland the early years of dieselisation in the London area saw a few successes but many failures and the maintenance staff were faced with de-rating the diesel engines of the troublesome classes in an effort to keep services running. Certainly in terms of reliability the Class 24s and 31s headed the statistics but even they were not without their problems. To some extent the railway operators and the commercial managers were to blame for some of the problems as they demanded more power in an effort to speed-up and upgrade services. At one stage the Class 31s were uprated to 1,600hp and in one case 2,000hp but generally such experiments had a serious effect on reliability. Eventually all of the Mirrlees engined Class 31s received English Electric diesel engines rated at 1,470hp.

There were two major developments in 1961 when the 1,750hp English Electric Type 3s — Class 37s — and the 3,300hp Class 55 'Deltics' were introduced. The Class 37s went to work on the GE lines and the Class 55s on the GN main line. In the meantime the venerable Class 40s had continued to improve their availability figures but they were under powered for the heaviest and fastest expresses on the ECML. With the arrival of the 'Deltics' the GN Class 40s were all transferred to Stratford. Even the 'Deltics' and the Class 37s had teething troubles but overall the ER had at last received diesel locomotives which earned a fine reputation over the ensuing years. During the early 1960s a number of 'one-off' prototypes were used on ER lines including the original Class 47 *Lion* and the hybrid diesel electric *Falcon*, which used high speed diesel engines linked to an electric transmission. These were followed in 1962 by the 2,700hp English Electric 'DP2', the predecessor of the Class 50s and the most successful of all the prototypes. Even the SR Class 33s made an appearance on the Cliffe-Uddington cement train which they worked to York, in the hands of ER crews.

Outside of the London and Eastern Counties area the East Midlands and South Yorkshire areas saw a heavy influx of diesels from about 1963 as the total number of Class 31s delivered exceeded 250. The production Sulzer Type 4s, Class 47s, were introduced from 1962 and the full tally of 200 Class 40s had also been delivered, although many of these were working on the LMR and ScR. Steam was quickly on the way out as the number of diesel locomotives in the ER fleet increased. In the north-east the unusual twin engined Class 17 'Claytons' had started to find work and they were supported by Class 24s and later Class 25s. Inter-regional passenger trains were often headed by the Class 45 'Peak' locomotives and later Gateshead was to have a sizeable stud of the Brush traction motored Class 46 'Peaks'. The Class 47s provided the main nucleus of motive power but they too had engine problems which was to result in the down rating of their 12-cylinder Sulzer engines from 2,750hp to 2,580hp.

Depots in the north such as Tinsley became fully operational during 1964. The pattern of freight traffic changed which resulted in little work for the diesel classes which could offer less than 1,100hp and modern block loads resulted in locomotives being fitted with air brakes and in the case of some Class 47s slow speed controls for the ever increasing volume of merry-go-round traffic. There were of course visits to the ER by many classes from other regions and there were diesel engined trains which received little limelight such as the small four-wheeled railbuses which were tried on very minor branch lines. The gradual dieselisation of the region took place as the number of new deliveries of what were to become BR's standard classes increased. In 1968 the last of the prototypes arrived on BR from the Hawker-Siddeley Company; the 4,000hp *Kestrel* but it ran only to the end of 1969 and was eventually sold to Russia. Diesel traction completely replaced steam on the ER during 1967 and with the completion of new locomotive deliveries the modern traction machines consolidated their position. All corners of the region were exclusively in the hands of the internal combustion engine, save for a little electrification out of Liverpool Street and in the Tyneside area, plus the eastern end of the 'Woodhead' route.

It was not until 1976 that another new class of diesel locomotive appeared. By this time most of the early non-standard and under powered classes had been withdrawn and BR were looking for a heavy freight engine. This arrived in the form of the 3,250hp Class 56 and by the early part of 1977 the class were being delivered to Tinsley in some numbers for use in the Shirebrook area, mainly on mgr trains. The prototype IC125 High Speed Train unit had made an appearance in the early 1970s and by 1979 the production Class 254 units had taken over several services on the ECML running not only between London and Newcastle/Edinburgh but also to Leeds, Harrogate and Hull, By 1982 the great majoritiy of ECML services were IC125 workings and even the mighty 'Deltics' had all been withdrawn. At the time of writing it seems that the IC125 units will be the ultimate development in terms of diesel traction on passenger trains and the only new class of diesel locomotive on the stocks will be the Class 58 freight engine.

Many of the original dmus dating back to the late 1950s are still running on the ER even though suburban electrification has been extended and many rural lines have closed. Various classes of shunter have come and gone but Class 03 and 08 locomotives are still busy at work on the ER. Class 50s are sometimes borrowed by the region after overhaul at Doncaster Works but on the debit side the older Class 40s and 46s are nearing the end of their lives. Diesel locomotives have now been at work on the ER for more than a generation and the photographs contained in this volume show a variety of classes at work throughout the region. The geographical area covered by this volume incorporates the old North Eastern Region and ranges from London in the south to Berwick in the north and from Lowestoft in the east to Hebden Bridge in the west.

By way of acknowledgement I would like to thank Gavin Morrison, Brian Morrison and Colin Marsden for putting their photographic collections at my disposal and to all other contributors who have assisted in providing material to enable me to produce a balanced appreciation of diesel traction in action on the ER during the past 25 years but with some emphasis on the last five years. The ER covers a massive area and in a little over 200 illustrations it has not been possible to include photographs of trains on every line. However notwithstanding the inevitable constraints on space I hope that *Diesels on the Eastern* will join similar Ian Allan books on the SR, LMR and WR on many enthusiasts' bookshelves.

John A. M. Vaughan
Goring-by-Sea, Sussex
October 1982

Lines in East Anglia

Top: One of the first lines on the BR system to receive series production main line diesel locomotives was the Great Eastern route from Liverpool Street to Norwich. Class 40s appeared on scheduled services from 1958. At the time of writing services are in the hands of the Class 47/4s hauling air conditioned coaches but the route is listed for early electrification. In this February 1978 view a steam heating Class 47/0 No 47.118 stands at the head of the 09.30 express for Norwich, which is composed of dual heating Mark 2a stock. *John Vaughan*

Above: Introduced as North British Type 1s the single cab Class 16 locomotives spent all of their short life allocated to the ER. Only 10 of the 800hp locomotives were built and the first example appeared at Stratford during 1958. By 1968 the class was extinct. A member of either the Class 15 or 16 fleet was often used as the Liverpool Street station pilot and No D8403 was photographed at the GER terminus in May 1959. *Martin Welch*

Right: When the Class 40s were introduced they were asked to compete with 'Britannia' class steam locomotives on the demanding two hour Norwich expresses and also on some trains working over the Clacton lines. The new 2,000hp diesels were found to have superior acceleration to a 'Pacific' steam locomotive but the 'top end' performance fell short of the best of the 'Britannias'. Passing Bethnal Green on 4 June 1958 is No D202 with the down 'East Anglian'. *Brian Morrison*

Below: Oil tankers and Freightliners make up much of the present day traffic at Ripple Lane Yards and most of the traffic is inter-regional. With the electrified line to Tilbury on the right No 47.192 uses all of its power to get a long line of four-wheeled tank wagons on the move and out of the yard in the up direction. Photographed on 31 October 1979. *Brian Morrison*

Above: There are two routes from London to Southend and consequently two stations at the well known resort. The line from Liverpool Street branches away from the GE main line at Shenfield and from the intermediate station of Wickford a branch to Southminster has survived. Several of the towns on the branch are now firmly established as bases for commuters. The green livery of the dmu dates this February 1970 view, taken at Woodham Ferres of a Wickford bound train. *John Vaughan*

Left: About 38½ miles from Liverpool Street is Witham, which is the junction for Braintree. There was once a further branch to Maldon but this closed to passengers during 1964. Running through the up fast road is Class 37 No 6727 (now No 37.027) with a Class 7 freight. Note the signal panel building on the right. *John Vaughan*

Top: The branch from Marks Tey to Sudbury once continued to Haverhill and Cambridge and also by a further branch line to Bury St Edmunds. However following cut-backs during 1961 and 1967 Sudbury became the terminus. The line has survived more that one threat of closure although operating losses continue. Waiting at the overgrown platforms on 28 May 1981 with the 15.34 to Colchester is Cravens unit Nos E56413 and E50383. *Brian Morrison*

Above: Colchester is an important railway centre which has its own motive power depot and a rich variety of trains serving Norwich, Parkeston, Walton and Clacton. In this view the daily March-Liverpool Street via Ipswich parcels train calls at the station with its load of half a dozen GUV vans. No 37.099 was photographed on 21 March 1981. *John Vaughan*

40 157

Left: This photograph was taken just five months before air conditioned coaches were transferred to the Norwich route from the WR. Passing the snow covered landscape at Ardleigh, between Colchester and Manningtree with the 09.30 Liverpool Street-Norwich on 29 November 1980 is No 47.179. Several of the Stratford Class 47s have been converted from Class 47/0 to Class 47/4 and this particular locomotive is now eth fitted No 47.577. *Michael J. Collins*

Below left: From Manningtree the important branch to Parkeston Quay and Harwich Town diverges and there is a triangular junction with the main line giving access in both the up and down directions. Parkeston is an important import/export centre and there is much inter-regional freight traffic. There was once a daily visit by a Class 40 from the north and on this day in March 1981 it was No 40.157 which ran through Wrabness station and passed an ancient GER coach body in the former goods yard. *John Vaughan*

Right: With Harwich just visible along the estuary in the background No 37.265 passes the home signal at Wrabness with an up train of empty 'Cartic' wagons. The line sees a rich variety of Freightliners, ABS (air-braked services) and Cartic traffic as well as the local dmu service and Parkeston Quay boat trains. These 'Cartics' are bound for Helsby on the Wirral. *John Vaughan*

Below: A rare and vintage scene at Ipswich. The engines are all green here as Brush Type 2 No D5594, now Class 31/1 No 31.174, occupies the middle road with the Hadleigh branch freight and English Electric Type 4 No D209, now Class 40 No 40.009, heads a Norwich-Liverpool Street express in June 1961. *Stanley Creer*

Above: Ipswich station stabling point carries the code IP, although in practice the depot does not now have a main line locomotive allocation, only a couple of Class 03 shunters to work the docks branch. This pair of Class 37s with two versions of split headcode panel rest on the stabling point at the weekend and are framed by a Class 03 and match wagon in the foreground. *John Vaughan*

Below: Norwich retained its semaphore signalling well into the 1980s and with a multitude of services to Ely, London, Yarmouth, Lowestoft, Birmingham and Sheringham there has always been sufficient movement to retain the interest of most enthusiasts. Curving away from Norwich Thorpe station with the 11.42 departure for London is No 47.100 on 5 February 1980. The lines to the left go to Whitlingham Junction and behind the now abandoned freight depot is the Wensum Curve (Norwich avoiding line). *John Vaughan*

Top: A delightful branch terminus with a tidy all over roof was Aldeburgh in Suffolk. Although this view was taken as recently as 1961 the scene is essentially the old order with a signalman controlling the infrequent train movements by his elderly lower quadrant GER signal. This Derby built dmu in original livery departs for the junction at Saxmundham. Services were axed forever during September 1966.
Stanley Creer

Above: East Anglia has always been renowned for its rural lines and branch freight, although by the 1980s this has dwindled to barely measureable amounts. In this quaint 1961 scene the Waveney Valley line freight from Beccles to Bungay headed by a 204hp Class 05 shunter arrives at Bungay. Passenger services ceased back in 1953.
Stanley Creer

Below: Diesel locomotives have now been working lines in East Anglia for more than a generation. The GE lines were one of the first areas to be converted from steam to diesel traction. In days before yellow warning panels appeared on locomotives a newly delivered No D6717 (later No 37.017) waits at the terminus of Lowestoft with a through train to Liverpool Street. *Stanley Creer*

Bottom: The north-east corner of Norfolk is well known for the 'Broads' waterways. A couple of pleasure craft can be seen in this view of the River Waveney near Haddiscoe. Many years ago a line to Yarmouth South Town from Beccles crossed the line visible here but that is now history. This Metro-Cammell two-car unit trundles between Norwich and Lowestoft during 1961. *Stanley Creer*

Above: The line to Great Yarmouth is busy on summer Saturdays but for the rest of the year the traffic mainly comprises a dmu service to Norwich via either the Berney Arms or Acle routes, and a handful of through trains to Liverpool Street, via Norwich. Heading some Mark 1 stock at Yarmouth Vauxhall on 27 August 1979 is No 37.075. In the background beneath the all-over roof is a Cravens dmu.
John Vaughan

Below: Brundall is the junction where the Yarmouth (direct) and Lowestoft routes divide. Passing the signalbox and about to make for Yarmouth with a Chartex special from Chichester and Worthing in West Sussex in August 1979 is No 47.180 *County of Suffolk*. This was the last train organised by the WSRTT which for 10 years had run special trains with the profits going to a number of charities.
John Vaughan

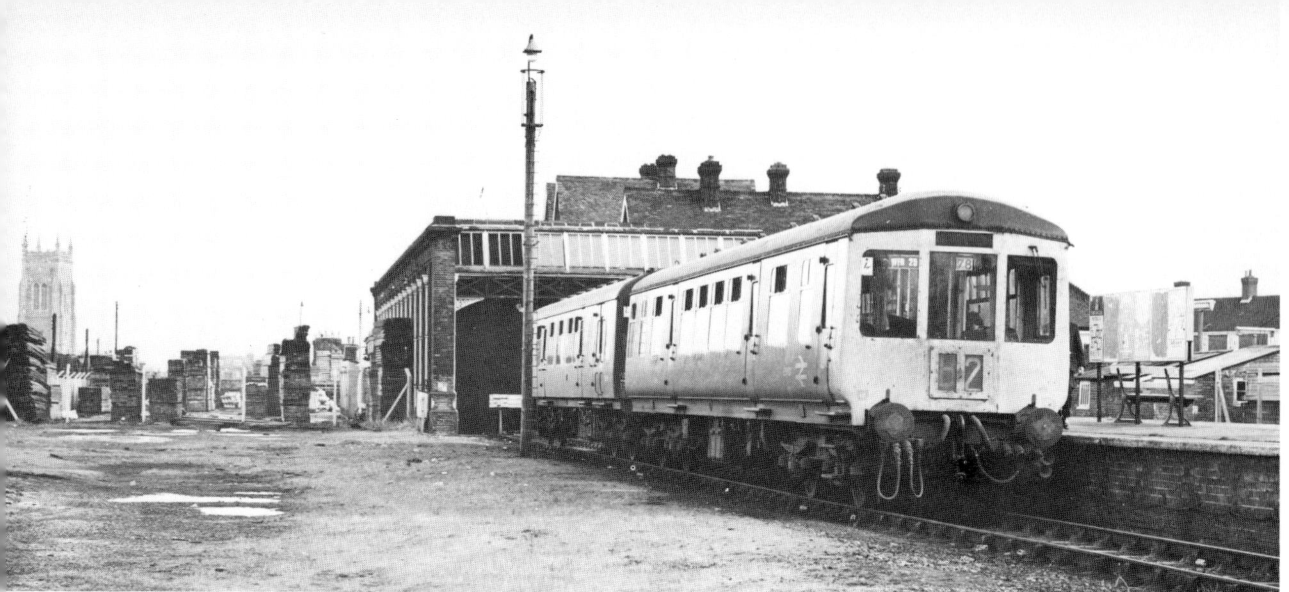

Top: Sheringham is another branch line survivor. About 10 trains per day in each direction travel the $30\frac{1}{2}$ miles between Norwich and the North Norfolk town. All Sheringham trains reverse at Cromer Beach station and travel over nearly four miles of the old Midland & Great Northern Joint Railway. One of the surviving Gloucester Class 100 two-car dmus stands at Cromer in January 1978. *John Vaughan*

Above: An interesting locomotive hauled working is the 12.40 Harwich-Peterborough service. Three or four ageing Mark 1 coaches and a couple of vans was the normal load during the latter part of 1980. Entering Bury St Edmunds station on 13 December 1980 is No 37.044. *John Vaughan*

Top: An extremely rare visitor to Bury St Edmunds on 10 March 1979 with the DAA 'West Riding Limited' tour from the SR to the ER was Plymouth Laira's No 50.050 *Fearless*. The 100mph interloper is seen during a photographic stop. The 'through roads' have been removed thereby reducing operating flexibility. *John Vaughan*

Above: Adding to the motive power variety on the Ely-Haughley Junction line are Class 25s Nos 25.269 and 25.301 passing Kennett station with the 09.48TThFO stone train from Mountsorrell-Kennett Redland Sidings on 3 October 1980. Through workings from the LMR and ScR often produce interesting locomotives on the line but the photographer needs to be very patient to capture such freight traffic on film. *John C. Baker*

Right: Towards the end of 1980 initial proving trials on the Leyland Experimental Vehicle had been completed and the first line to be used as a 'guineapig' for the new device was the East Suffolk line between Ipswich and Lowestoft. However in this November 1980 view LEV was being used on a Cambridge-Bury St Edmunds special and is seen near Kennett Redland Sidings. *John C. Baker*

Below: On Saturdays when Ipswich football club is playing at home, the usual early afternoon dmu service from Cambridge is normally replaced by a locomotive and stock. In this January 1981 shot No 31.305 pauses at a rationalised Newmarket station with the 12.50 ex-Cambridge. The old station building has been demolished and only single track is now provided. *John Vaughan*

Below right: The normal East Anglian motive power of Class 31, 37 and 47 locomotives are nowhere to be seen in this view of Thetford station. Stealing the limelight is SR 'Crompton' Class 33 No 33.019 which had arrived from the SW Division of the SR with a troop train. The SR crew worked the train throughout with a pilotman. *Colin Marsden*

Left: The other main route out of Liverpool Street is to Cambridge. The line gained in importance when the direct Kings Cross-Cambridge trains were withdrawn from the ECML and all through traffic was concentrated on the former GER route. In the London suburbs at Tottenham South Junction No 31.231 heads an up freight to Temple Mills Yard in January 1982. *John Hicks*

Below: The overhead electrification ends at Bishops Stortford at the time of writing although the Cambridge line is a logical candidate for further electrification which would link-up with an extension of the electrified line from Hitchin to Royston. For the time being the setting at Stansted is charming as this study of No 37.084 on the 16.00 Kings Lynn-Liverpool Street shows. Note the interesting goods shed, the semaphore signal, signalbox and lattice overbridge — all signs of the railway of yesteryear. *John Vaughan*

Top: Elsenham was once the junction for Thaxted but branch services ceased over 30 years ago. Although on the main line Elsenham still has manually controlled crossing gates and original station buildings. On 28 July 1981 No 31.112 heads the 15.36 Liverpool Street-Cambridge stopper into the station. *John Vaughan*

Above: There is still a modicum of freight on the GE Cambridge line but the days of the local pick-up goods have long gone. On the brighter side a new siding has been installed at Duxford between Great Chesterford and Whittlesford to serve the CIBA factory there. Hauling chemical tankers away from the works is No 31.268. *John Vaughan*

Above left: Stratford depot was up to its old tricks to commemorate the Royal Wedding in July 1981. No 47.583 *County of Hertfordshire* was painted in 'union jack' red, white and blue. Storming through Whittlesford with the 10.36 Liverpool Street-Kings Lynn is the striking locomotive which also sports black window surrounds, grey roof and silver buffers. *John Vaughan*

Left: A superb ganty at Whittlesford has defied modernisation. Passing the dainty lattice work of Whittlesford's home signal support is No 37.041 heading the 09.27 Cambridge-Liverpool Street on a glorious morning in July 1981. The goods yard still receives a daily train of chemical tankers but the old commodities of farm produce and coal have gone on to the roads. *John Vaughan*

Above: A very tall signal at Swavesey overlooks the daily sand train on the St Ives (Cambs) branch line. Train 8L42 rumbles along the branch in April 1970 behind No 6746 (now No 37.046). Passenger trains ceased just six months after this photograph was taken but the line has survived to Fen Drayton just short of the old St Ives station site, for this mineral traffic. *John Vaughan*

Above: There is a forest of semaphore signals in the Ely area. Just north of the station is Ely North Junction where a complicated track layout directs trains which can approach the area from five directions. In this view No 47.018 leaves Ely's frost covered sleepers behind with the 08.36 Liverpool Street-Kings Lynn on 8 December 1980.   *Michael J. Collins*

Top right: Kings Lynn is now effectively the end of the direct line from Liverpool Street and the town still enjoys a two hourly service to the Capital. Many lines once radiated from the area but all have now closed to passengers except the main line. One of the few branch line survivors kept open for freight traffic is the line to Middleton Towers, where British Industrial Sand is loaded into old-generation hopper wagons. Creeping along the old Dereham line is No 37.009 on 15 April 1981.   *Michael J. Collins*

Right: In September 1968 a Class 7 freight of empty coal wagons was photographed passing March East Junction. Before the advent of fully fitted freights diesel locomotives often had the assistance of a brake tender to halt their loads within the distance required by the length of the signalling sections over certain routes. No D6723 (now No 37.023) was then in green livery. Note how busy the yard in the background was in those more prosperous days.
John Vaughan

From Kings Cross to Doncaster

Above: The number of photographs in the Kings Cross area is unproportionally high to show the wide variety of locomotives which have visited the terminus and some of the rarer early classes now departed from the scene. Early Class 40 workings included the 'Master Cutler' to Sheffield and the 'Yorkshire Pullman' and No D201 (No 40.001) is seen entering Kings Cross sporting an express passenger headcode during 1959. *Martin Welch*

Below: The prototype DP2 looked every inch a 'Deltic' and yet 'underskin' it was effectively the original Class 50, employing a single large slow revving diesel engine as distinct from the two high speed engines of the Class 55s. The machine was highly successful until it met an untimely end in an accident during July 1967. Leaving Kings Cross with a down Pullman train in August 1965 DP2 is about to enter Gasworks Tunnel. *BR*

Left: The start of the classic journey from Kings Cross to Edinburgh Waverley is alway filled with expectation which commences when the locomotive is about to back on to the train. In July 1966 a 'Deltic' in green livery but by then with small yellow warning panel emerges from Gasworks Tunnel and backs on to the 'Flying Scotsman'. The colour light signals seen here have now been replaced, the track layout streamlined and the sky has been filled with wires. *John Vaughan*

Below: The buffer stops at Kings Cross must rival the sea wall at Dawlish as qualifying for the most hackneyed photographic location in the country. But suddenly with the passing of time a basic photograph of one extinct and one near redundant class of locomotive side by side becomes of interest. On 17 January 1981 an early morning scene finds No 55.004 *Queens Own Highlander* beside Gateshead's No 46.048; both having worked up with overnight trains. *John Vaughan*

Above: During the days when the operators were prepared to go out of their way to accommodate the railway enthusiast the opportunity was taken to charter one of the fast disappearing Class 52 'Western' diesel-hydraulics for a run from Kings Cross to York. This view shows No D1023 *Western Fusilier* at the end of its return run with the WLA 'Western Talisman' on 20 November 1976.   *John Vaughan*

Left: The track configuration on Holloway Bank has changed considerably over the years and now concrete abutments carry 'flyover' lines from the up to the down side of the outer approaches to Kings Cross. On a day when trains were diverted from the LMR's St Pancras route into Kings Cross No 45.129 made a rare appearance with an express for Sheffield. Photographed at Copenhagen Tunnel on 2 June 1981.   *Brian Morrison*

Above: One of the early classes of Type 1 diesel was the British Thomson-Houston 800hp Class 15. A total of 44 locomotives were built from 1957 but the entire class were withdrawn between 1968 and 1971. The main reason for their demise was the changing pattern of BR traffic and their under-powered disesel engine. A few locomotives survived to become train heating units. Here No ADB968003 stands in front of four 'Deltics', led by No 55.015 *Tulyar*, at Finsbury Park depot. *John Vaughan*

Below: A scene transformed out of all recognition is the view from the platforms of Finsbury Park station looking north. Passing between No 5 and No 6 signalboxes is one of the 10 Class 23 'Baby Deltics'. The class were introduced in 1959 for use on the GN suburban network. The locomotives were beset by failures and they had all disappeared by 1963 for extensive modifications to be carried out. They re-appeared in traffic but never quite made the grade being withdrawn finally during 1971. *English Electric*

Top: Another rarity, this time near Harringay, when a WSRTT Chartex from West Sussex worked through the North London suburbs behind its SR motive power in the shape of double headed Class 33s, with No 33.052 leading. The organisers remove the 'White Rose Limited' headboard before a Class 47 takes over the train. The train had joined the ECML at Harringay West Junction. *John Vaughan*

Above: Potters Bar was one of the first stations to be modernised on the ECML following the take over of former LNER lines by BR(E). In this previously unpublished photograph of the prototype 'Deltic'; the blue, white and gold locomotive is heading the 12.20 Hull-Kings Cross on 28 February 1959. The following year the original 'Deltic' was retired to the science museum. *J. N. Faulkner*

Right: The driver of this Class 47/4 will not need to worry about the 105mph restriction as he hurries his 95mph mount towards London on 25 August 1981. Quite often the Class 47s substituted for non-available 'Deltics' and such was the case on this day. No 47.410 leaves Welwyn South Tunnel with the eight Mark 2d/e coaches which it has worked up from York. *Michael J. Collins*

Below: By January 1982 IC125 units had taken over the great majority of ECML services and only a handful of overnight trains and the occasional working to Cleethorpes remained locomotive hauled, with the exception of the Peterborough commuter services. Speeding through Stevenage with the 17.50 Kings Cross-Leeds on 5 April 1981 is No 254.030. The unit numbers are now being painted over with only the tiny power car number available for identification. *Brian Morrison*

Above: One of the few freights able to find a path on the IC125 infested ECML passes Ardesley, north of Hitchin on 19 November 1979 behind No 31.225. The train of empty 'Grampus' wagons is bound for the pw engineers depot just south of Hitchin station on the up side of the line.
John Vaughan

Below: The 1,470hp Class 31s have been associated with the Peterborough commuter eight-coach sets for many years. Despite the lack of power this train, the 07.42 from Peterborough, takes just one hour to reach Kings Cross with a single stop at Huntingdon. No 31.230 passes Langford, a few miles north of Hitchin. *Colin Marsden*

Top: An interesting scene at Sandy, Bedfordshire. At precisely 09.32 on 2 May 1979 No 25.132 works some very ancient wooden wagons full of ballast towards Hitchin on the up relief line. On the right is the trackbed of the old Oxford–Cambridge line which crossed the ECML by an overbridge, now demolished. The cross-country line between Bedford and Cambridge, via Sandy, closed from 1 January 1968. *John Vaughan*

Above: One of the last Class 55 'Deltics' to survive was No 55.009 *Alycidon*. In May 1979 it was reasonable to expect a 'racehorse' on the 15.40 Leeds–Kings Cross and sure enough the high pitch note of its Napier engines heralded the approach of 'number 9'. The formation is passing Abbots Ripton, just north of Huntingdon. *John Vaughan*

Left: During 1980 the Finsbury Park 'Deltics' had their window surrounds painted white, which for the photographer made the FP machines fairly distinctive and recognisable from a considerable distance. With the customary plumes of exhaust No 55.007 *Pinza* leaves Peterborough with the 14.05 ex Kings Cross on 27 May 1980. *John Vaughan*

Below: A general view of the new Peterborough station. In the old days all trains had to slow to 20mph through the station but now three figure speeds can be attained. With a Class 37 locomotive and a down IC125 unit in the background No 56.068 heads a Ratcliffe-Fletton fly-ash train through the complex of lines. *John Vaughan*

Right: Hauling a long unfitted freight out of Peterborough Yard is No 31.206 of March depot. Peterborough once had two large engine sheds at New England Yard and Spital Bridge but all it can boast nowadays is a stabling point. The Class 31s were introduced in 1957 with 1,250hp Mirrlees diesel engines but during the mid-1960s these were removed in favour of the 1470hp 12-cylinder English Electric 12SVT engine. *John Vaughan*

Below right: Just north of Peterborough the former Midland Railway and Great Northern Railway tracks run parallel to each other. The MR line to Stamford and Melton Mowbray is used mainly by the infrequent trains between Birmingham and Norwich. Passing the old disused goods shed at Helpston is No 31.244 on 19 September 1981 with the 13.15 from New Street. The ECML can be seen behind the Class 31. *John Vaughan*

Left: A locomotive destined to be painted in green livery and ultimately preserved was No 55.002 *The King's Own Yorkshire Light Infantry*. On 8 September 1979 it was diagrammed to work the 10.05 Kings Cross-York, a regular 'Deltic' turn in their final years of service. The heavier than usual train is passing Little Bytham in Lincolnshire. *John Vaughan*

Below left: Little Bytham station closed during 1959 on the ECML route and the old M&GN station closed earlier in the same year. In this photograph the bridge abutments on the old M&GNJR route from Bourne can be seen just to the left of the rear power car of the IC125 unit. Passing the site of the GN station is No 254.023 with the 09.10 Harrogate-Kings Cross. *John Vaughan*

Right: Another abandoned station site is at Essendine where lines once crossed and joined the ECML from both Stamford and Bourne but both were closed to passengers during the 1950s. With the passengers of 12.05 Kings Cross-Hull sitting in air conditioned comfort without sparing a thought for the railways of the past No 55.006 *The Fife and Forfar Yeomanry* speeds northwards with little effort in September 1979. *John Vaughan*

Below: One of the last trains on the ECML to retain non-air conditioned stock was the 09.40 Kings Cross-Edinburgh summer service. This was also the last daytime Anglo-Scottish locomotive hauled working out of London. On 20 June 1981 No 55.013 *The Black Watch* arrives at Grantham station, junction for Nottingham and Skegness. *John Vaughan*

Right: Although the autumn of 1981 undoubtedly belonged to the 'Deltics' how wonderful it was to see another 20-year old veteran lumbering up the ECML. Running between Barkston South Junction and Peasecliffe Tunnel, north of Grantham with a parcels train for Peterborough on 19 September 1981 was No 40.121. The sight brought back memories of the early days of dieselisation when the Class 40s were active on crack expresses.
John Vaughan

Below: Powering an unidentified train through Barkston Junction at 13.18 on Saturday 19 September 1981 was 'Peak' No 46.014 with a down seven-coach train. The Class 46s regularly appeared on the ECML but never in large numbers. At times their steam heating capability was invaluable on overnight trains but such a facility will be of no value at all with the withdrawal of steam heated rolling stock.
John Vaughan

Above: An old blue enamel sign still proclaims that the derelict building on the left is Newark's British Railways Goods Depot. No 55.004 *Queen's Own Highlander* arrives at the Nottinghamshire station with the 15.50 York-Kings Cross, which was the photographer's means of transportation back to London. *John Vaughan*

Below: A view at Newark station which few people see. This bay platform faces the up direction on the down side and was probably used before World War 2 by trains running to Bottesford Junction. Standing in the adjacent sidings with a brake van is Class 08 shunter No 08.277. *John Vaughan*

254 023

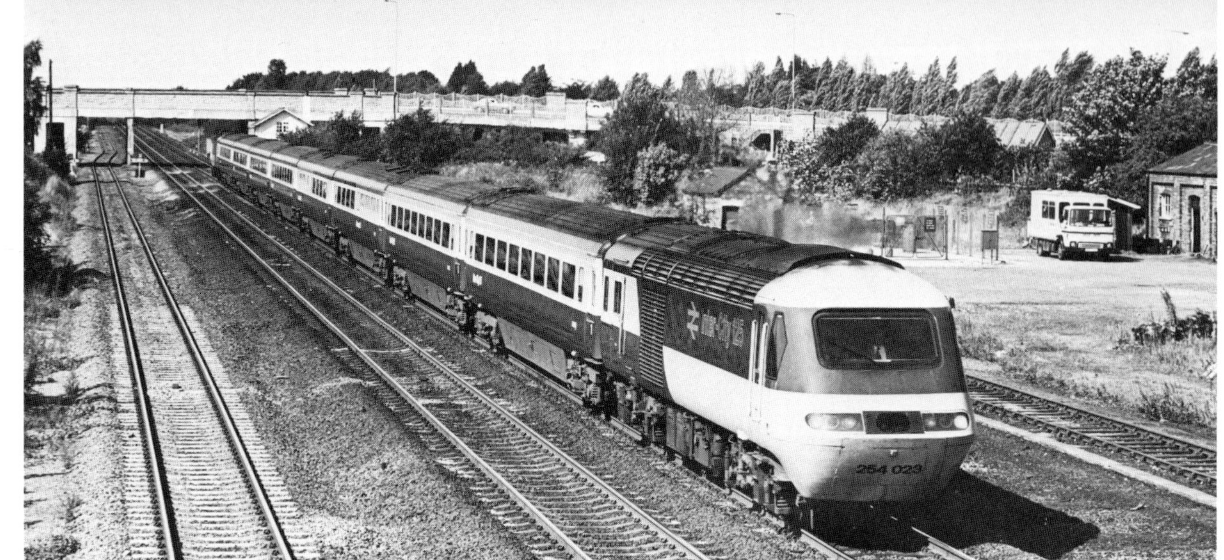

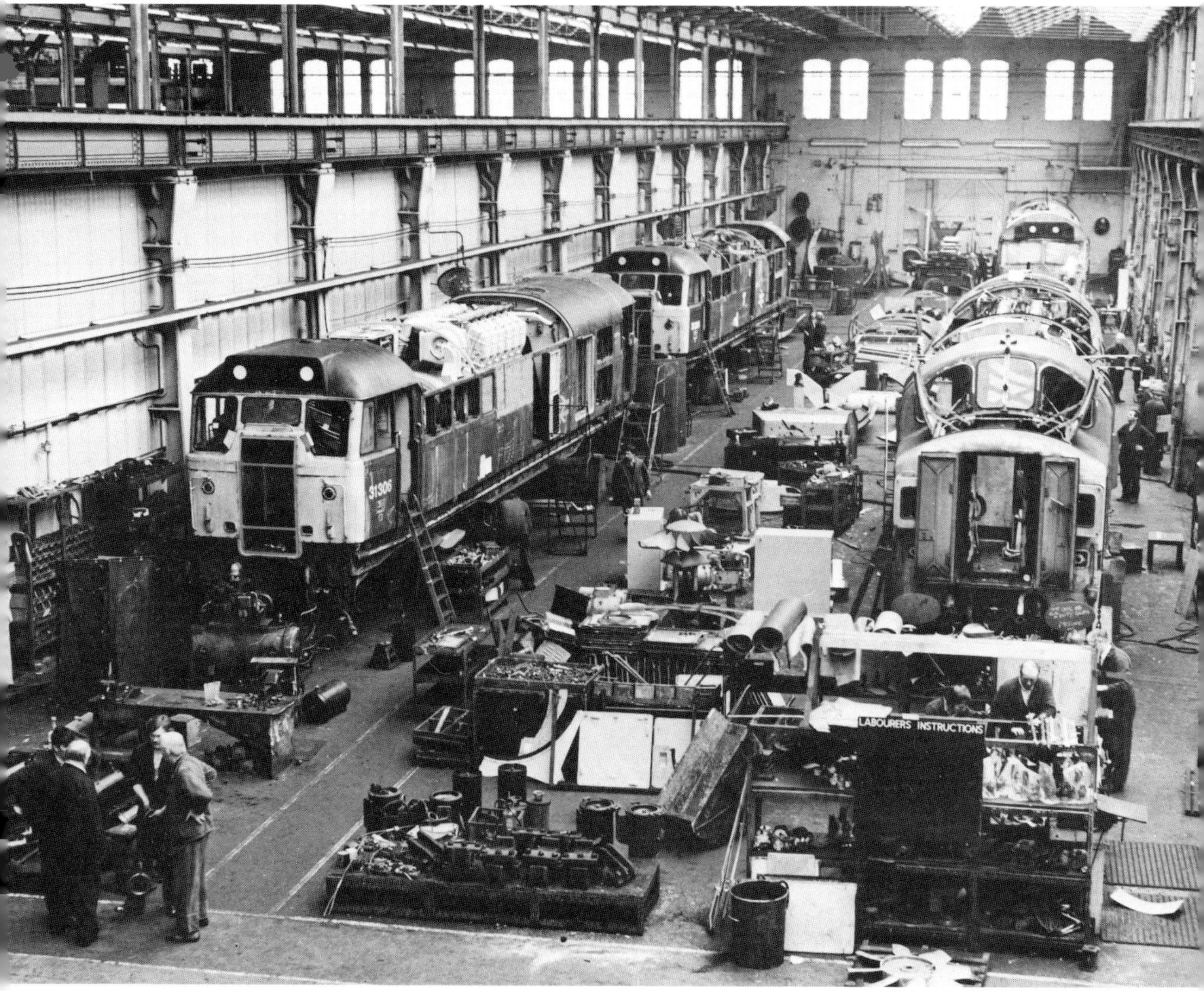
31306
LABOURERS INSTRUCTIONS

Above left: North of Newark, junction for Lincoln, the next stations and location of any significance is Retford, where passengers may change for Sheffield or stations in the Gainsborough direction. Flying towards the station is the up 'Flying Scotsman' on 6 September 1980 with IC125 No 254.023 in standard eight trailer coach formation. *Brian Morrison*

Left: Doncaster has always been an important railway centre. Not only is Doncaster a railway junction but one of the major BREL Locomotive Works is located in the town, adjacent to the BR station. Class 03, 13, 31, 37, 50 and 56 are overhauled at the Works and until recently Class 56s were constructed there. This work has now been transferred to Crewe but Doncaster will take over Class 58 construction. In this general view No 31.306 has just received a new engine and behind are other machines from the English Electric stable. *John Vaughan*

Above: When the 'Deltics' were still running in BR service Doncaster had the responsibility for heavy maintenance. They are also in the process of refurbishing the whole of the WR Class 50 fleet. The locomotives visible in this October 1980 view from left to right are: Nos 08.401, 56.002, 50.004 *St Vincent*, 56.014 and 55.019 *Royal Highland Fusilier*. *Colin Marsden*

Below: Many of the BREL and formerly BR Workshops scrap old locomotives as well as building and overhauling the new and in-service machines. No 10800 was an 827hp diesel electric prototype which appeared from the North British Works in 1950. At the end of its days the locomotive languished in Doncaster Works but it was not scrapped. It was returned to the Brush Works and eventually emerged as their research locomotive named *Hawk* but still carrying its original running number. *Derek Porter*

Above: Two classes of locomotive to be scrapped at Doncaster were the SR Class 71 and 74 locomotives. Not all of the locomotives were scrapped at 'The Plant' but these examples were among the last survivors. Class 74 electro-diesel No 74.010 stands in front of the all-electric Class 71 No 71.004 on 10 August 1980. *John Vaughan*

Right: No 40.038 is framed by the huge letters of the 'BREL Engineering' sign in front of Doncaster Works. The train is heading north and the load is grain travelling from rural East Anglia or Lincolnshire. Class 40s are now being withdrawn in large numbers and it is predicted that these 2,000hp monsters will all be out of service by the end of 1984. *John Vaughan*

Above: The three-way junction north of Doncaster station. Swinging off the Scunthorpe line with a mixed freight are a pair Class 20s, or 'Choppers'. Straight ahead is the main line to York and Edinburgh while on the left are the lines to Leeds. In the background is a freight using the Doncaster avoiding lines to gain access to the Goole and Scunthorpe lines. Nos 20.009 and 20.154 were photographed on 23 April 1981. *Colin Marsden*

Left: A powerful telephoto lens shows the three routes mentioned in the previous caption more clearly, at least in respect of track layout. Taking to the lines leading to the platforms of Doncaster station indicates that this 'Deltic' will be stopping to set down/pick up passengers. No 55.014 *The Duke of Wellington's Regiment* was photographed on the 15.50 York-Kings Cross on 26 July 1981. *John Chalcraft*

Lincolnshire and South Humberside

Above left: The railways of the Fenland have always been under photographed and yet train workings have always been particularly diverse. Stamford is just inside the ER boundary and so this photograph is fully entitled to a place in this volume. Passing the former MR station on 10 October 1981 with the 13.16 Norwich-Birmingham is No 31.293. *Michael J. Collins*

Left: Spalding has had an interesting history and a glance at the Ian Allan 1923 Gazetteer reveals that railways approached the town from no less than six directions involving three different railway companies. With the closure of the GN&GE Joint line in 1982 Spalding became just a 'one line' through route with a very sparse passenger service. The one day of the year when Spalding really comes to life is when the annual Flower Festival is held when specials arrive in considerable numbers. On 12 May 1979 SR No 33.044 arrives with an Adex special from Ramsgate in Kent. *Les Bertram*

Above: The last 'Deltic' to call at Spalding was No 55.009 *Alycidon* which was heavily delayed due to the absence of a guard and bad weather on the 'Deltic Broadsman' rail tour in December 1981. The delay allowed participants to photograph the train during the unscheduled stop. The combination of sun and snow was superb. *John Vaughan*

Top: With resorts such as Skegness and to a lesser extent Cleethorpes there is much holiday traffic on summer Saturdays. Honington Junction is located just to the east of Barkston Junction. A branch line once ran from here to Lincoln via Leadenham. Alas it is no longer a junction and the weeds grow higher on the long closed station platforms. Running past the immaculate signalbox for the very last time on 5 September 1981 is the 14.20 Yarmouth-Derby headed by a pair of Class 25s, Nos 25.274 and 25.323.
John Vaughan

Above: One of the joys of summer Saturday traffic in the area for a number of years has been the use of non-boilered freight engines on passenger trains. Normally it is very rare to find a brace of 'Choppers' on Class 1 duty but even in the summer of 1981 one or two trains could be relied upon for Class 20 haulage. The most regular working was the 09.23 Derby-Skegness. The train is nearing Ancaster during the 1981 summer headed by Nos 20.157 and 20.088.
John Vaughan

Above: Passing the pristine station of Ancaster on 5 September 1981 is the 08.51SO Leicester-Skegness. It is doubtful that the old Mk 1 stock is of the dual heating variety and thus the provision of an eth locomotive in the shape of 'Peak' No 45.124 is unnecessary. Nevertheless the 1Co-Co1 locomotive makes an impressive sight between the GNR signalbox and goods shed.   *John Vaughan*

Below: The driver of this dmu seems to be making a gesture at the photographer in this beautifully lit picture taken at Grand Sluice Junction, Boston. The eight car formation gives a clue to the time of year. On 30 August 1980 the 09.54 Skegness-Grantham has Derby Class 148 car No E56018 leading. Note the signalman has already lowered the home signal above the right hand bridge girder.   *Brian Morrison*

Above: A typical Fenland skyscape is a suitable background for this shot of an excursion from Alfreton and Mansfield Parkway to Skegness headed by Nos 20.139 and 20.048. The pair are passing the attractive Heckington Mill on 27 August 1979. Judging by the weather participants will have a pleasant day at the seaside. *John C. Baker*

Left: One of the most easterly lines in Lincolnshire was the Mablethorpe branch. In common with Skegness the line saw mainly dmu traffic except on weekends in the summer when locomotive hauled holidays trains would arrive with passengers from the northern industrial cities. Leaving the single track at Willoughby Junction and joining the Grimsby-Louth-Firsby 'main' line is a Class 31 working a Mablethorpe-Sheffield train during 1969. There is no railway here at all now. *John Vaughan*

Below: The Firsby-Lincoln line was a favourite of the author's. The sleepy rural atmosphere of the whole area was perpetuated in the local train service. Trains were few and far between which makes this scene at Woodhall Junction look unbelievably busy. A two-car dmu working from Sheffield to Skegness leaves the station and passes the daily Horncastle branch freight headed by green Class 31 No D5678 (now No 31.250) on 11 July 1969. The freight is waiting for the road to Lincoln. *John Vaughan*

Right: A really quaint photograph which shows the condition of the Horncastle branch in April 1970. This picture was taken just months before the end and looking at the crumbling wooden sleepers and the wooden keys the track clearly dated back to GNR days. One of the less common Class 10 Blackstone engined shunters, No D4075 (now scrapped) heads two empty tankers past a remote farm crossing south of Woodhall Spa station. The branch closed to passengers in 1954 and to freight in 1971. *John Vaughan*

Below: Lincoln is another major junction of minor and secondary railway lines. The County has suffered badly from line closures and the loss of freight traffic. For the present both Lincoln St Marks and Lincoln Central stations survive but there are plans to rationalise. Leaving Lincoln Central on 28 July 1979 with the 08.35 Newcastle-Yarmouth is No 31.173. *Gavin Morrison*

Above: Grimsby Town station has the unusual feature of a modern all over roof incorporated in a much older station building. The tendency has always been to demolish the all over roof. One of the curious Class 123 dmus with No E52098 leading leaves Grimsby for Cleethorpes with a train from Sheffield on 19 April 1980. In the centre road is No 08.751. *John Vaughan*

Below: The original New Holland Town station and the short stub to New Holland pier closed when the new Humber suspension bridge was opened during 1981. The buildings, signs and general paraphernalia had been untouched for years. Pausing at the old Town station is an enthusiasts special from Gloucester headed by double-headed Class 20s Nos 20.029 and 20.028. *John Vaughan*

Above: A mixed livery dmu stands at the branch terminus of Barton-on-Humber on 19 April 1980. Nearly all of the passenger traffic in the area is in the hands of dmus except the occasional through train from Cleethorpes and Grimsby to Kings Cross. There is, however, heavy freight traffic in the Immingham Dock area, about 12 miles from this location. *John Vaughan*

Top right: Trying to satisfy the insatiable appetite for coal of the power station at Keadby is this loaded mgr train of HAA hopper wagons. The train is coming from the Doncaster direction and is passing Crowle on 14 July 1981. Behind Class 47/3 No 47.310 is the Stainforth and Keadby canal. The load has come from one of the pits in the Pontefract area. *Stanley Creer*

Right: There are two massive British Steel Corporation plants at Frodingham, near Scunthorpe. They make their contribution to railfreight in the area and this train of steel girders is a good example. In this impressive view 'Peak' Class 45/0 No 45.015 crosses the bridge at Althorpe station on its way towards Doncaster, on 29 October 1980. *Colin Marsden*

Between Selby and Newcastle

Above: The resplendent product of BREL Doncaster. Ex-works No 37.023 heads the works test train along the down line at Chaloners Whin Junction, near York on 10 May 1980. Before an ex-Works locomotive can be returned to traffic it must undergo proving trials to see whether any gremlins appear. This quite often involves a run to Newcastle and back with a rake of Mark 1 stock or a line of former LMS parcels vans. *Gavin Morrison*

Left: A Class 40 on freight duty at Dringhouses Yard, south of York had failed on 9 September 1981 and had to be rescued by a Class 47. Heading for Healey Mills, near Wakefield are Nos 47.277 and 40.015 (formerly *Aquitania*) with a lengthy mixed freight. There seems to be a lot of space in the yard behind. *Colin Marsden*

Above: A period piece dating back to the days when the Class 27s worked south of the Border and indeed were allocated to depots from Finsbury Park to Thornaby. On 16 June 1962 a pair of 1,250hp Class 27s Nos D5374 and D5377 use the York avoiding line with an up freight. No D5374 was later converted for push pull working and was renumbered No 27.101 and No D5377 is now No 27.030. *Gavin Morrison*

Below: During November 1981 the Plymouth-Edinburgh through train went over to IC125 operation but before that the southbound working was often used to transfer Class 50s from Doncaster Works to Plymouth, Laira. Such was the case on 18 April 1980 when No 50.007 *Hercules* received some minor but important attention at Doncaster and then departed with 1V93. The 'Hoover' is basking in the sunshine at York. *Roger Kaye*

Above left: The magnificent station roof at York is seen in almost silhouette in this photograph of a Scarborough bound dmu at the north end of the station. The Scarborough lines can be seen disappearing to the right in the background. York is a fine railway centre and near to the station is the National Railway Museum which now houses a good selection of modern traction as well as steam exhibits. *John Vaughan*

Left: Up and down 'Deltics' at York during their last five months of service. In this Sunday scene in August 1981 No 55.008 *The Green Howards* approaches the south end of York station with the 16.05 from Kings Cross while in the right foreground No 55.004 *Queen's Own Highlander* waits departure with the 19.13 York-Kings Cross. *John Chalcraft*

Top: The line north of York is straight and almost level and it has always had a reputation as a racing ground. There are now only two intermediate stations between York and Darlington, namely Thirsk and Northallerton. Passing Thirsk on the down slow line is No 25.046 on 13 June 1974 with a freight for the Newcastle area. *Brian Morrison*

Above: In pre-IC125 days the Class 55 'Deltics' always stole the limelight on the ECML but undoubtedly the class which have put in the greatest overall mileage is the '47s' (unfairly nicknamed 'Duffs'). With over 500 locomotives in the class their appearances should be regular, especially as many are allocated to the ER. On a typical express of the 1978 period No 47.406 (now named *Rail Riders*) presses-on through Ferryhill with a down working. *Gavin Morrison*

Left: The ancient City of Durham is a fine location to view passing trains and a magnificent viaduct is located just south of the station. The view towards the Cathedral with rows of terraced houses in the foreground is spectacular. At 16.08 on 13 May 1980 a Class 45/0, which has been demoted from the ranks of express passenger locomotives by its lack of eth facilities, rolls over the viaduct with southbound hoppers. The locomotive is No 45.022 *Lythan St Annes*. *John Vaughan*

Top: At Durham the accent is on variety and the long succession of freight trains provide full time entertainment for enthusiasts interested in the modern scene. There is 3,500hp available to the driver of this brace of Class 37s working in multiple which are entering Durham station from the north. The leading machine is No 37.015 and the date is 13 May 1980. *John Vaughan*

Above: Making steady progress towards its destination of Tyne Yard is No 31.181 which is just coming off the two-track viaduct and is making use of the down through road at Durham station. The two-track section continues through Chester-le-Street to Ouston Junction where four tracks allow express trains to get past the many slow freights in the area. *John Vaughan*

Above left: No 50.010 *Monarch* (seen here before naming) is a very long way from its home base of Plymouth Laira. On 9 August 1977 the 100mph locomotive had just been outshopped from Doncaster Works and was photographed at Ouston Junction, South of Tyne Yard with a down test train. The train has just swung across to the slow lines and the lines in the right background lead to Consett.
Ian S. Carr

Centre left: Newcastle's main diesel depot is Gateshead and only recently has its importance reduced with the concentration of IC125 units at Heaton. The small Class 03 shunters are used as station pilots around Newcastle Central and their size is exaggerated by the bulk of 'Peak' No 46.056 in the background. Featured here are Nos 03.069 and 03.059 photographed from a passing train in May 1979.   *John Vaughan*

Below: A 1970 scene at Newcastle Central station. A 'Peak' has just come to a halt with inter-regional passenger train 1E32 while around the back of the station sneaks No 31.160 with a mixed Class 4 freight. All means of train identification were lost from 1976 when the train codes were abandoned and yet, ironically the codes are still used in the 1982/3 working timetables.
John Vaughan

Above: In the good old days when north-east/south-west services were hauled by the massive 138-ton 'Peak' class locomotives and when Bristol Bath Road had an allocation of Class 46s No 46.020 of BR waits to leave Newcastle Central with a train for the West Country. The 'Newcastle' sign in front of the engine is in the old orange and white livery of the short lived North Eastern Region. *John Vaughan*

Left: The modern Newcastle Central with only multiple units in the shape of diesel mechanical units and IC125 formations with not a locomotive to be seen. The Cravens unit on the right is leaving with the 11.01 to South Shields and on the left No 254.017 is arriving with the 09.15 from Edinburgh Waverley, on 29 May 1980. *Brian Morrison*

Routes to the Humber, Tees and Wear

Above: There are many interesting and under photographed lines to the east of the ECML in the Counties of Humberside, North Yorkshire, Cleveland, County Durham and Tyne and Wear. From the south the main access to the Goole and Hull areas is via Doncaster and Stainforth Junction. Passing Stainforth with an eastbound coal train on 29 October 1980 are Nos 20.212 and 20.228.   *Colin Marsden*

Top right: With the modern NCB Hatfield Colliery in the background No 47.216 passes Stainforth and Hatfield station with a train of empty mgr HAA hopper wagons for loading at a Dearne Valley colliery. This particular locomotive was involved in a number of incidents and to avoid superstition amongst train crews it was renumbered No 47.299 in the early months of 1982.   *Colin Marsden*

Right: The modern image at Goole with IC125 unit passing automatic lifting barriers illuminated by high slender lamp posts and controlled by mas colour light signals. The 12.35 from Hull rushes towards Doncaster and Kings Cross on 13 July 1981. In the background are dock cranes in the port beside the River Humber.   *Stanley Creer*

Top: This Class 47 is coming off the Goole line and is about to join the Hull-Selby line at Gilberdyke Junction. The former NER route is now the only surviving east/west route to Hull, the old Hull and Barnsley line having expired many years before. No 47.461 was heading the 08.05 Kings Cross-Hull on 21 April 1980. *Gavin Morrison*

Above: Some 500 enthusiasts on the RPPR's 'Hull Hornet' enjoyed a photographic stop at Brough, just over 10 miles from Hull, on 13 October 1979. The locomotives provided to take over from No 47.078 *Sir Daniel Gooch* at Doncaster were Nos 37.252 and 37.221, both of Immingham depot. The train had originated in London. *John Vaughan*

Above: The most powerful diesel engine to run on BR metals was No HS4000 *Kestrel* which was introduced by a Brush/Hawker Siddeley consortium during 1968. The 4,000hp locomotive turned the scales at 126 tons and the Sulzer engine was capable of propelling the stylish prototype along at speeds of 125mph. It was withdrawn and sold to Russia, by the owners Brush Electrical in 1971. In this scene the locomotive is at Hull Dairycoates shed on 18 April 1970. *Norman E. Preedy*

Below: There is still a reasonable amount of freight activity in the Hull area although the fishing industry and the docks generally are not as busy as they once were. Other than for minor freight lines the two main passenger routes are to Selby/Goole to the east and to Scarborough to the north. curving into Hull on 31 August 1980 with the 12.05 SuO from Kings Cross is No 55.014 *The Duke of Wellington's Regiment. Brian Morrison*

Top: The ghostly appearance of one of Hull's Class 03s is due to repeated chemical treatment through the carriage washing plant. With the renovation and redecoration of the overall roof nearing completion No 03.075 hauls the stock from the working shown in the previous photograph out of the station to release the locomotive. *Brian Morrison*

Above: Malton and Seamer are the only intermediate stations on the $42\frac{1}{4}$-mile line from York to Scarborough. Malton is yet another station which was once a four-way junction but is now a minor station on a single through route. The marvellous train shed has survived the passage of time and approaching Malton in this September 1980 shot is the 12.19 York-Scarborough four-car dmu, Nos E50644, 59247, 59381 and 50645. *Brian Morrison*

Above: Scarborough is a well known Yorkshire resort on a quite rugged part of the north-east coastline. In common with such towns as Yarmouth and Skegness and railway traffic is very lively on summer Saturdays. The station track and platform layout is very interesting with double and single faced platforms and bays of various lengths. This 1970 view shows a Metropolitan-Cammell dmu at platform 4.
John Vaughan

Left: Beneath a fine array of semaphore signals just outside of Scarborough station No 31.135 waits to leave with the 13.30SO to Sheffield Midland while No 03.189 fusses about with two empty coaches, on 2 August 1980. Adjacent to the main station is a special holiday platform and a small oil terminal. *Gavin Morrison*

Right: There was once a spectacular coastal route linking Scarborough with Whitby, a distance of about 22 miles. However to travel between the two places now involves a rail journey via York, Darlington and Middlesbrough, a distance of over 136 miles! Running beside the River Esk near Whitby is the 10.13 to Middlesbrough on 27 May 1980, comprising Class 101 unit Nos E50181 and E51236.
Brian Morrison

Below: Part of the massive Tees Yard is visible in this scene. Double headed Class 37s, Nos 37.007 and 37.001, two of some 40 locomotives of the class allocated to Thornaby, move gingerly forward with some huge BSC iron ore hoppers in May 1980. Most of the modern freight wagons are now air braked or vacuum fitted and loose coupled workings with brake vans are becoming a thing of the past.
Brian Morrison

Above: The prototype Class 252 IC125 unit was making test runs during 1973 and by 1975 the WR were evaluating the unit's potential. No 252.001 formed part of the Stockton & Darlington Railway's 150th anniversary celebrations and participated in the Shildon 150 parade. On 27 September 1975 the Duke of Edinburgh travelled to Eaglescliffe to attend celebrations in Preston Park. Here No 252.001 nears Stockton-on-Tees in pouring rain for stabling. *Ian S. Carr*

Below: Stockton station once boasted a fine all over roof but by May 1979 it was being demolished. The roof looks to be in a sorry state in this view taken with a telephoto lens from a RPPR special to Consett. The Class 37 then travelled over the freight only route from Norton South Junction to Ferryhill on the ECML. *John Vaughan*

Above: The coastal route from Darlington to Newcastle via Sunderland is fascinating. There is uneasy co-existence between freight and passenger trains, although the latter are now almost entirely dmus. In this period piece 'Peak' No D182 (later No 46.045) passes underneath Church Street signalbox, West Hartlepool with the 11.05 Newcastle-York parcels on 8 June 1967. Note the green livery and the LNER 'Gresley' buffet car.
John M. Boyes

Centre right: A Royal train at Horden, County Durham on 25 June 1963. About to leave Horden station with a special conveying HM The Queen Mother is No D274 (now No 40.074). Shortly after this photograph was taken the coastal stations of Easington, Horden and Blackhall were closed, leaving only Seaham open between Sunderland and West Hartlepool.
Ian S. Carr

Below right: This light 72ton Class 25 needed the assistance of a brake tender to safely control this long coal train from Seaham. These Bo-Bo locomotives were not really successful on such duties. No D5184 (now No 25.034) approaches Ryhope Grange Junction on 10 May 1966.   *John Vaughan*

Above: There are a large number of collieries along the north east coastal line and there were several branches between the sea and the Leamside line. In this remarkable picture No D5107 (later No 24.107 — now scrapped) nears Silksworth Colliery on some decidedly 'dodgy' track with wagons from South Dock (Sunderland). The photograph was taken is March 1969 and two years before this it would have been a 'J27' class steam engine on this turn. *Ian S. Carr*

Below: No D5102 (No 24.102) takes the Biddick Lane line at South Pelaw with a Consett-Tyne Dock train of iron ore empties on 19 November 1966. At this time some ore trains were single headed by Class 24 or 25 locomotives between Tyne Dock and South Pelaw where a banker (normally a Class 40) was attached for the long climb to Consett. All workings have now ceased with the closure of the Consett Steel Works. *Ian S. Carr*

Right: The final day of activity at Cox Green before closure. One of the curious 'Clayton' Class 17 locomotives, No D8592, heads a Class 8 Pallion-Tyne Yard freight through the station in torrential rain. After 18 August 1967 the Penshaw North-Hylton section was taken out of use. *Ian S. Carr*

Below: Many of the interesting lines in the area have now been closed and lifted and to show diesel traction in the area means using photographs which were taken some years ago. Running up the Leamside line from Washington with a loose coupled freight, 9P12, on 31 August 1964 is No D8595. The Class 17s had two 6-cylinder 450hp engines and 117 locomotives were built. They were introduced from 1962 but half the class were withdrawn in 1968 and by 1972 they were extinct, at least on BR metals. *Ian S. Carr*

Top: On 13 April 1972, when this photograph was taken, Class 31 No 5527 (No 31.109) was a relative newcomer to the north-east. Passing Penshaw North is a fitted vacuum braked train of magnesian limestone. The Leamside line was temporarily closed during 1979 due to earthslips and an underground fire. *Ian S. Carr*

Above: There was once another complex of lines in the Bishop Auckland and Consett areas but the present BR map reveals that only the line to Eastgate Works from Bishop Auckland survives. Another blow to the area was the closure of the BSC Consett Works in 1980. Not long before closure No 37.062 runs over lines at Consett which, sadly have outlived their usefulness. *John Vaughan*

Trains in Derbyshire, Nottinghamshire and the Sheffield Area

Top left: West of the ECML the ER/LMR boundaries can be found just south of Chesterfield station and just south of Shirebrook, in the East Midlands coalfields. Just north of Chesterfield, in Derbyshire, No 45.145 heads the up 07.58 Leeds-St Pancras on the former Midland Railway main line and passes No 20.019 on an engineer's ballast train. *John Vaughan*

Left: When photographed on 17 June 1980 the sight of an IC125 unit at Chesterfield was something of a rarity. No 253.012 was on a test run after overhaul at BREL's Derby Works. However from the autumn of 1981 a number of inter-regional train using this route ceased to be locomotive hauled and High Speed Train sightings here became a daily occurrence. *John Vaughan*

Above: Near Chesterfield is the large BSC Staveley Works. There are also a large number of collieries in the area. Passing Foxlow Junction, just east of Staveley is 'Whistler' No 40.086 with a westbound train of steel bars in railfreight wagons. Barrow Hill depot is nearby. *John Vaughan*

Right: This Class 45/0 'Peak No 45.029 has now been withdrawn but on 18 June 1980 it was certainly going well with eastbound coal empties near Clipstone West Junction. The train was initially bound for Mansfield Concentration sidings. This part of the ER system once belonged to the lamented Great Central Railway. *John Vaughan*

Below: The old GCR route to Lincoln has now been severed at High Marnham, to the east of Tuxford on the ECML. This piece of track is now used solely by mgr trains working to and from High Marnham Power Station. Returning towards Dukeries Junction with empty HBA hoppers is No 56.010. *John Vaughan*

Left: Whitwell station on the Midland Railway line from Mansfield to Worksop closed in 1964 although the nearby colliery and quarry are still open. Passing a typical MR signalbox with coal empties is No 31.270 on 12 December 1979. The line sees considerable mgr traffic which serves West Burton and Cottam power stations. *Colin Marsden*

Below: The mgr duties in the area are shared between Class 47 and 56 locomotives although the latter are favoured because they can haul four additional 50 ton hoppers and they have sanding gear which assists adhesion in some of the tricky colliery sidings. On 17 June 1980 No 47.302 leaves Cottam power station and heads towards Retford with mgr empties. *John Vaughan*

Right: A heavy load of 34 hoppers with an all up weight of almost 50 tons each means this Class 56 has earned its keep on the climb up to Clarborough Tunnel, east of Retford. Slowing for the junction into West Burton power station is No 56.017. Like many other Class 56s this locomotive is allocated to Tinsley, Sheffield but in fact it spends most of its time at Shirebrook depot. *John Vaughan*

Below: Passing through the unloading chute on its 'merry-go-round' circuit of West Burton power station is No 56.017 on 17 June 1980. For this purpose the locomotive will have its slow speed control activated which means that the driver can proceed automatically at speeds varying from $\frac{1}{2}$–3mph. Millions of tons of coal are now transported by this very efficient method. *John Vaughan*

Top: Nearing the site of the former Retford South Junction with up coal empties from the Gainsborough direction are Nos 31.264 and 31.271. The train is making for Worksop. This east-west line once crossed the ECML at Retford on a level crossing set at right angles with the main line but this was replaced by a 'flyunder' during the late 1960s.
John Vaughan

Above: No 47.601 was an interesting hybrid which was used as a testbed for what was to become the diesel engine for the Class 56 locomotives. In 1975 No 47.046 was converted to accommodate the 3,250hp 'mill' and reclassified Class 47/6. On 28 February 1977 No 47.601 leaves Treeton Junction, Sheffield with an up mgr train.
Gavin Morrison

Left: Passing the solid looking upper quadrant signals at Treeton Junction in quite appalling climatic conditions on 15 November 1979 is this Class 37 heading a mixed freight towards Tinsley Yard. The lines to the right go to Treeton North Junction and Rotherham. Colour light signalling has now been introduced. *John Vaughan*

Below: During 1965 three pairs of Class 08 shunter were converted into 'master and slave' units specifically for hump shunting in Tinsley Yard, near Sheffield. This effectively produced a 700hp unit with all the advantages of availability associated with the normal Class 08s. As is obvious in this view of part of Tinsley the cab of one of the units was completely removed during conversion.
John Vaughan

Right: Excitement on 1V93 on 26 September 1980 as No 50.003 *Temeraire* powers out of Sheffield and makes for Dore and Chesterfield after overhaul and refurbishment at BREL Doncaster. This was only the second Class 50 to be painted in the new style livery which particularly suits the class, at least when the locomotive is clean. *Roger Kaye*

Below right: No 40.113 had just run round its train at Sheffield Midland station when photographed on 17 January 1981. The veteran had worked in on a parcels train from Cleethorpes, although the load included some passenger coaches. The locomotive retains its original headcode disc indicators. *John Vaughan*

Above: An eth fitted Class 45/1 brings the 11 bogie 07.40 Cardiff-Newcastle into Sheffield Midland. Sheffield has tended to be the poor relation in its rail communications with London and even in 1982 much of the route has manual signalling and it will only be in October 1982 that a handful of IC125 units stray on to the former MR main line. Other trains such as the Harwich-Manchester and Nottingham-Glasgow trains reverse at the station before continuing along the Hope Valley line. *John Vaughan*

Below: Just to the north of Sheffield Midland station is Nunnery Carriage sidings. There is a short branch behind the sidings, from Woodburn Junction and taking this line on their way to Tinsley Yard are Nos 20.210 and 20.015 on 19 May 1981. The sidings and part of the city are in the background. *John Chalcraft*

Above: An unusual movement past Woodburn Junction
signalbox on 13 November 1979. A brace of Class 08
shunters, Nos 08.539 and 08.208 negotiate the curve
leading to Tinsley Yard. The locomotives are under the
1,500Vdc electrified system of the 'Woodhead' lines which
was finally switched off in July 1981.   *John Vaughan*

Below: To the north-east of Sheffield is Rotherham and
Wath. Lines to Leeds, York and Doncaster all go their
separate ways in the area. Passing Rotherham Road with a
long unfitted train of coal empties on 31 October 1980 are
Nos 20.132 and 20.001. The train is destined for Wath
Yard.   *Colin Marsden*

Left: A very fine photograph showing the northern approaches to Rotherham Midland station. Passing the now demolished signalbox at Masborough Station North with the 12.35 Leeds-Birmingham is 'Peak' No 45.067 (now withdrawn) on 28 February 1977. With changes to signalling, non-eth locomotives, '0000' headcode panels, Mark 1 stock and on the right jointed bullhead rail this scene is already historical. *Gavin Morrison*

Centre left: Class 20 haulage is as popular as ever on this RPPR rail tour in June 1978. In fact there were so many customers for a visit to Doncaster Works from the London and Birmingham areas that two trains had to be run and four Class 20s provided. In this scene Nos 20.186 and 20.187 pause at Mexborough with one of the 'Doncaster Detour' trains. *John Vaughan*

Below: In years gone by Wath Yard was part of the Great Central Railway and the area has always been a mecca for coal trains of every description. Traffic has gradually dwindled as today's mgr trains run direct from the pit to the power station and marshalling is not required. Amidst miles of old four-wheeled wagons No 37.119 eases out of the yard with a southbound freight. *Colin Marsden*

Above: On the nearby main line is Wath Road Junction. Working hard on 19 May 1981 is No 46.009 with a Tyne Yard–Washwood Heath, Birmingham freight. The second vehicle is a siphon G Enparts van marked 'to work between Gateshead TMD and Swindon Works only'. At the time of writing this locomotive is one of the few Class 46s still running. *Clive Jarrad*

Left: In a regional book it is of course not possible to show pictures of every line, especially in South and West Yorkshire where there are so many freight only lines. However it was not possible to resist this view of ex-Works Class 50 No 50.035 *Ark Royal* keeping the residents of Cudworth awake with its distinctive beat as it powers 1V93 Edinburgh-Plymouth past Cudworth North Junction on 5 May 1981. *John Fozard*

Lines in South and West Yorkshire

Top: Wakefield Kirkgate station belonged to the Lancashire & Yorkshire Railway. It once enjoyed the benefits of an all over roof which would have been useful on such a day as seen in this photograph. Making for Healey Mills with an up coal train on 15 November 1979 is No 37.096. Wakefield Westgate is now the main station for Leeds or London. *John Vaughan*

Above: A pleasant study of the open countryside around Normanton. No 25.205 heads a particularly mixed freight southwards up the Midland Railway route. The train will take either the Wakefield or Sheffield line at Goose Hill Junction. In the background is Altofts Junction where the lines to Leeds and Castleford divide. Note the colour light and the semaphore signals on the same post. Photographed on 20 August 1980. *John Vaughan*

Above: No 56.034 has stopped right outside of Knottingley diesel depot to change crews with a loaded mgr train for the mighty Drax power station. In the early part of 1980 the 3,250hp Class 56s gradually replaced the 2,580hp Class 47s at Knottingley as payloads increased. *John Vaughan*

Below: Propelling some spoil wagons over the little used spur connecting the freight only Shaftholme Junction-Knottingley line with the Knottingley-Goole line in a south to east direction is No 40.058 on 20 August 1980. The spur is just behind KY depot. This 'Whistler' has had its headcode discs removed. *John Vaughan*

Left: Eggborough power station has its own double track line leading off of the Knottingley-Goole line at Whitley Bridge. At nearly 17.30 hours the mgr traffic is still running as No 56.027 heads some empties, HAA hoppers, back to the pits beyond Pontefract Monkhill. The freight only Class 56s rarely see carriage washing plants and accordingly, they are in very grimy condition. *John Vaughan*

Below left: Running along the GN main line between Wakefield and Doncaster at Hemsworth is No 40.007 hauling a dead Class 313 emu No 313.026, on 25 March 1981. The tracks of the old Hull and Barnsley route to Cudworth crossed the GN at this point. The emu was being returned to London after attention at Horwich Works. *John Fozard*

Above: The lengthy $69\frac{1}{2}$ft bulk of this Healey Mills allocated Class 40 is evident from this picture showing No 40.187 curving into Horbury cutting with an eastbound mixed freight. The stores van next to the locomotive is a splendid old rigid wheelbase six-wheeler. This locomotive is one of the last to be built and it carries a black central headcode panel which once contained a route indicator blind. *John Vaughan*

Below: Making an exit from another of the north's major yards, Healey Mills, is No 37.104 with a loose coupled load, on 20 August 1980. Healey Mills also has a large diesel depot containing a rich variety of motive power, although in common with other depots it is well stocked only at weekends. *John Vaughan*

Top: With the sunshine and superb visibility illuminating the West Yorkshire hills around Mirfield split headcode box Class 37 No 37.031 hauls a mixed freight towards Huddersfield on 18 September 1979. Although York-Liverpool main line trains pass this point the local station is served mainly by Huddersfield-Wakefield dmus. *Gavin Morrison*

Above: Heaton Lodge Junction is where the freight only link between the Standedge/Diggle trans-Pennine route and the Sowerby Bridge route branches off. The line is invaluable as a diversionary line, normally at weekends. Coming off the freight line on 22 July 1980 is Nos 37.165 and 37.055 with a down oil train. *Gavin Morrison*

Above: It is not possible to couple one of the new generation emus to normal rolling stock without using a special match wagon. This Class 313 unit is far away from the GN suburban system as it passes Heaton Lodge Junction behind No 31.303. No 313.006 was on its way to works still showing its destination as Welwyn Garden City. *Gavin Morrison*

Below: The other ER approach to the Huddersfield area is from Sheffield and Penistone. Between Wath and Penistone and Sheffield and Penistone the line was part of the 1,500Vdc 'Woodhead' electrified system. This volume is confined to diesel traction and it was therefore necessary to obtain photographs of diesels under the wires. Passing Elsecar Junction with empty mgr hoppers is a named 'Peak' No 45.022 *Lytham St Annes.   John Vaughan*

Left: At Deepcar there are some exchange sidings where a BSC industrial shunter takes over from BR's locomotives. To assist in operations a resident Class 08 is stabled in the area. In very wintry conditions No 08.266 fights for grip on the approach to Deepcar sidings. The overhead electrified system was abandoned in July 1981.   *John Vaughan*

Above: When photographed on 26 February 1981 No 37.054 was invading Class 76 territory as it ran past the old disused platforms of Deepcar with an up engineer's train. The locomotive is heading a 'shark' brake van and large ballast hoppers towards Sheffield. The line on the left goes to the BSC Stocksbridge Works.   *John Vaughan*

Below: This photograph was taken from a train passing Huddersfield Junction near Penistone. No 31.309 was on an engineer's train but the reason for the particular interest was the old wooden panelled Gresley coach coupled to a LMS brake van behind the engine. Photographed on 13 October 1979.   *John Vaughan*

Above left: When the original 'Peaks', the 2,300hp
Class 44s, were being withdrawn a number of enthusiasts
specials were run. On 1 October 1977 it was the DAA/DEG
'Peak Express' which paused at Penistone before a run over
the Woodhead route. No 44.008 is seen here during a
photographic stop but other members of the class were used
on other stages of the journey.   *John Vaughan*

Left: The passenger services from Huddersfield to Sheffield
and from Huddersfield to Clayton West are hanging-on by a
thread. Shepley is the junction station for the doomed
Clayton West branch and in this wet January 1981 scene a
small group of passengers huddle together to board the
13.04 Huddersfield-Sheffield five-car dmu, which is showing
the incorrect destination of Wakefield Westgate.
John Vaughan

Above: There is still a small colliery adjacent to the Clayton
West branch passenger terminus which receives trains
about twice a week. On 5 August 1977 No 37.040 was
turned out for the duty and the 1,750hp Co-Co is seen at
Park Mill shunting coal wagons. Note the miniature snow
ploughs below the buffer beam.   *Gavin Morrison*

Right: The line from Penistone joins the trans-Pennine
Diggle route at Springwood Junction, Huddersfield. In this
quite splendid picture No 40.124 is passing the junction and
its 16-cylinder engine is just about to erupt, judging by the
dense exhaust coming from the exhaust ports. The 09.35SO
Newcastle-Manchester was photographed on 27 June
1981. Note the little 'English Electric' headboard which was
probably positioned by some Class 40 'bashers'.
Gavin Morrison

Above: Carriage labels have been used to identify this train.
1E86 proclaims the 09.00 Llandudno-York holiday train
which was running briskly down the bank at Haithwaite,
near Huddersfield behind No 25.196 on 21 August 1976.
The Class 25s are gradually disappearing from the scene and
especially on passenger workings, one of the last bastions
being the Cambrian Coast lines.   *Gavin Morrison*

Below: To the north of the Diggle route is the line over the
Pennines via Sowerby Bridge. The ER/LMR boundary is just
west of Hebden Bridge. Passing a typical industrial Pennine
scene is No 47.088 *Samson* with a diverted 12.20
Newcastle-Liverpool train, at Sowerby Bridge on
23 September 1979.   *Gavin Morrison*

Above: Whereas the Diggle route was the London & North Western Railways main artery from east to west the Sowerby Bridge line was Lancashire and Yorkshire territory. Emerging from the tunnel at Sowerby Bridge is one of the workhorses of the north, No 40.183 with a down freight freight on 25 July 1980. *Gavin Morrison*

Left: In the heart of the Pennines at Hebden Bridge stands No 40.044 after arriving with a special for enthusiasts visiting the Keighley & Worth Valley Railway on 22 March 1980. No 40.044 retains its headcode discs but the connecting doors on the front end have been replaced by a single sheet of metal, presumably following accident damage. *Gavin Morrison*

Above: Returning towards the Leeds/Bradford area this magnificent view shows scenery so typical of the West Riding of Yorkshire. The train may be 20th century but the buildings are mostly Victorian as 'Peak' No 46.033 from Gateshead coasts down the hill near Batley with the 10.02 Newcastle-Liverpool on 8 July 1976.
Gavin Morrison

Left: In the Bradford area there are hundreds of acres of derelict land which was once occupied by railway sidings to serve industry but particularly the textile and cotton mills. Passing buildings of yesteryear at Laisterdyke is a Class 47/4 heading the 11.55 Bradford-Kings Cross away from the city, in March 1978.
Gavin Morrison

Right: The old Bradford Exchange station was demolished and the land sold in the early 1970s and a new functional but featureless structure was built. Entering the new station just before Bradford-Kings Cross services were taken over by IC125 units is No 47.405 with a train from London.
Gavin Morrison

Above: The 'other' Bradford station and the poor relation to Bradford Exchange is Forster Square. Passenger traffic here is normally restricted to dmus but on 8 July 1979 the former Midland Railway terminus had its great day when Bradford-Kings Cross trains were diverted via Shipley. No 254.012 passes some parcels vans and the signalbox with the 08.23 to Kings Cross. *Gavin Morrison*

Below: Working a two-car Morecambe-Bradford train into Keighley is Class 101 Metropolitan-Cammell unit No E50198 during June 1978. Keighley has become well known in railway circles for the preserved K&WVR line to Oxenhope but its lesser known claim to fame is that it is the last station on the line before LMR territory starts. The station awning had been demolished shortly before the photograph was taken. *John Vaughan*

Above: Making for the Settle and Carlisle line is 'Peak' No 45.110 hauling the 10.31 Nottingham-Glasgow express past Hirst Wood, Shipley on 16 February 1981. From May 1982 all Anglo-Scottish working over the MR route via the S&C were diverted through Manchester. This train would once have run through from St Pancras and be called the 'Thames-Clyde Express'. *Gavin Morrison*

Left: The 27 December 1981 was a memorable day for many railway enthusiasts. The end of the Class 55 'Deltics' was celebrated by rostering two members of the class on Trans-Pennine workings on the last Sunday of their existence. Here No 55.009 *Alycidon* with suitable headboard and wreaths enters Leeds City station with the 12.05 Newcastle-Liverpool. *John Chalcraft*

Top left: Leeds Holbeck was a great depot in the days of steam but its importance gradually diminished and this situation was exacerbated by the decision to concentrate IC125 activities on Leeds, Neville Hill depot. Passing the Holbeck area with the Bradford Forster Square-Manchester Red Bank parcels is No 25.133 on 24 March 1979. *Gavin Morrison*

Left: Passing Wortley Junction, to the west of Leeds with the down 'Leeds Executive' on 28 July 1980 are IC125 units Nos 254.003 and 254.007. The lines to the right go to Holbeck East Junction and link-up with the main route to London through Wakefield Westgate. All Leeds-London and some inter-regional workings are now in the hands of IC125 units. *Gavin Morrison*

Above: A charming scene near Hunslet, south east of the City of Leeds. Looking a little like a train on a model railway Class 08 shunter No 08.224 probably feels very important as it heads a transfer freight past Hunslet in the up direction on 18 June 1979. *Gavin Morrison*

Above: Plunging into the well known Marsh Lane cutting on the North Eastern Railway's exit from Leeds is No 47.423 with the 12.17 Newcastle-Liverpool train on 18 April 1980. This 180-mile journey takes over four hours which is unattractive to the businessman who may find the M62 Motorway much quicker. However the rail journey is difficult with little opportunity for fast running over the Pennines or through our great cities. *Gavin Morrison*

Top right: Passing Bolton Percy between Church Fenton and York is this ultra-lightweight freight which can hardly be an economic working with 2,940hp of Class 31 up front. Nos 31.175 and 31.171 were photographed on 13 January 1981. Note that the leading locomotive has its number stencilled on to the headcode panel. *John Fozard*

Right: Harrogate is now on a loop line from Leeds to York, although in days gone by a main line continued north of Harrogate to join the ECML near Northallerton. Dmus run around the loop line but the main liners from Leeds terminate at Harrogate. Leaving Harrogate with the up 'Yorkshire Pullman' on 28 June 1977 (the last year of this named train) is No 31.410. *Stanley Creer*

The Far North-East Railroutes

Above: An interesting and under-photographed line in the north-east is the Benton-Ashington mineral line between Holywell and Earsdon Junctions. On 21 November 1980 Nos 37.063 and 37.073 power a Tynemouth-Low Fell coal train past Earsdon signalbox. The lines in the foreground (right) lead to the Tyne and Wear Metro test track. *Clive Jarrad*

Left: There is still an interesting freight line complex in the Blyth area. Most traffic joins the main line at Morpeth Junction. On a pleasant June evening in 1974 a Class 37 and brake van leave Blyth Yard and make for the diesel depot. One of the inlets from the North Sea can be seen on the right. *John Cooper-Smith*

Above right: On the freight lines just south of the River Tyne but west of the ECML is No 37.066 which is picking up a load of coal at the NCB sidings at Swalwell Colliery on 14 January 1981. Note the rows of terraced houses in the background with the more modern 'semis' on the higher ground. *Clive Jarrad*

Right: The ER has responsibility for most of the Newcastle-Carlisle route. The first major station along the route is Hexham where branches diverged to Allendale and Reedsmouth. No 40.062 waits in the loop with a Tyne Yard-Carlisle Kingmoor freight as a two-car Metro-Cammell dmu on a Carlisle-Newcastle working scuttles by. Note the interesting signalbox behind. *John Chalcraft*

Above: Haltwhistle was, until 1976 when the branch closed, the junction for Alston. Branch trains used the island platform on the right. Far removed from inter-city workings is this Wickham trolley and two trailer vehicles belonging to the engineer's department. The formation roars towards Newcastle on 8 September 1981. *John Chalcraft*

Right: The collapse of the Penmanshiel Tunnel during 1979 resulted in many diversions over the Newcastle-Carlisle route which included some 'Deltic' hauled trains. One of the lesser known Class 55 workings in later years was the 15.57 Carlisle-Edinburgh via Newcastle train. On 8 September 1981 No 55.013 *The Black Watch* was employed on the train which is seen passing Blenkinsop, near Haltwhistle. *John Chalcraft*

Above: Passing through some splendid Northumberland countryside near Slaggyford on the Alston branch is a Class 101 dmu. The crumbling dry-stone wall adds dimension to the scene. The Alston branch hung-on under threat of closure for many years but it finally succumbed in May 1976. *Stanley Creer*

Below: Curving through Morpeth with the Teesside Haverton Hill-Grangemouth ICI train No 6S41 is No 40.037, one of the Class 40s which has now been withdrawn. Some of the load will also end up at Leith, near Edinburgh. The photograph was taken on 22 June 1981. *Barry J. Nicolle*

Right: Further up the coast at Alnmouth, formerly the junction for Alnwick, the 13.00 Kings Cross-Edinburgh IC125 service with No 254.014 leading passes the station and makes for Berwick on 29 May 1980. The station is served by a sparse local service from Newcastle and a single overnight train in each direction on the Edinburgh-Kings Cross run. *Brian Morrison*

Centre right: With the North Sea just visible in the right background No 47.421 passes Scremerston, south of Berwick in sparkling form with the 15.10 Edinburgh-Kings Cross on 10 June 1978. The station here was closed back in 1951 which indicates the size of the local community. All principal trains are now formed of IC125 units over this part of the ECML. *Gavin Morrison*

Below: The Eastern Region meets the Scottish Region just north of Berwick-upon-Tweed and it is fitting to end our 'railtour' of the ER with a view of the Royal Border Bridge. Passing over the craggy stonework of the 100ft high curved viaduct above the River Tweed is No 46.034 heading the four bogie 08.10 Newcastle-Edinburgh Waverley, on 30 May 1980. *Brian Morrison*

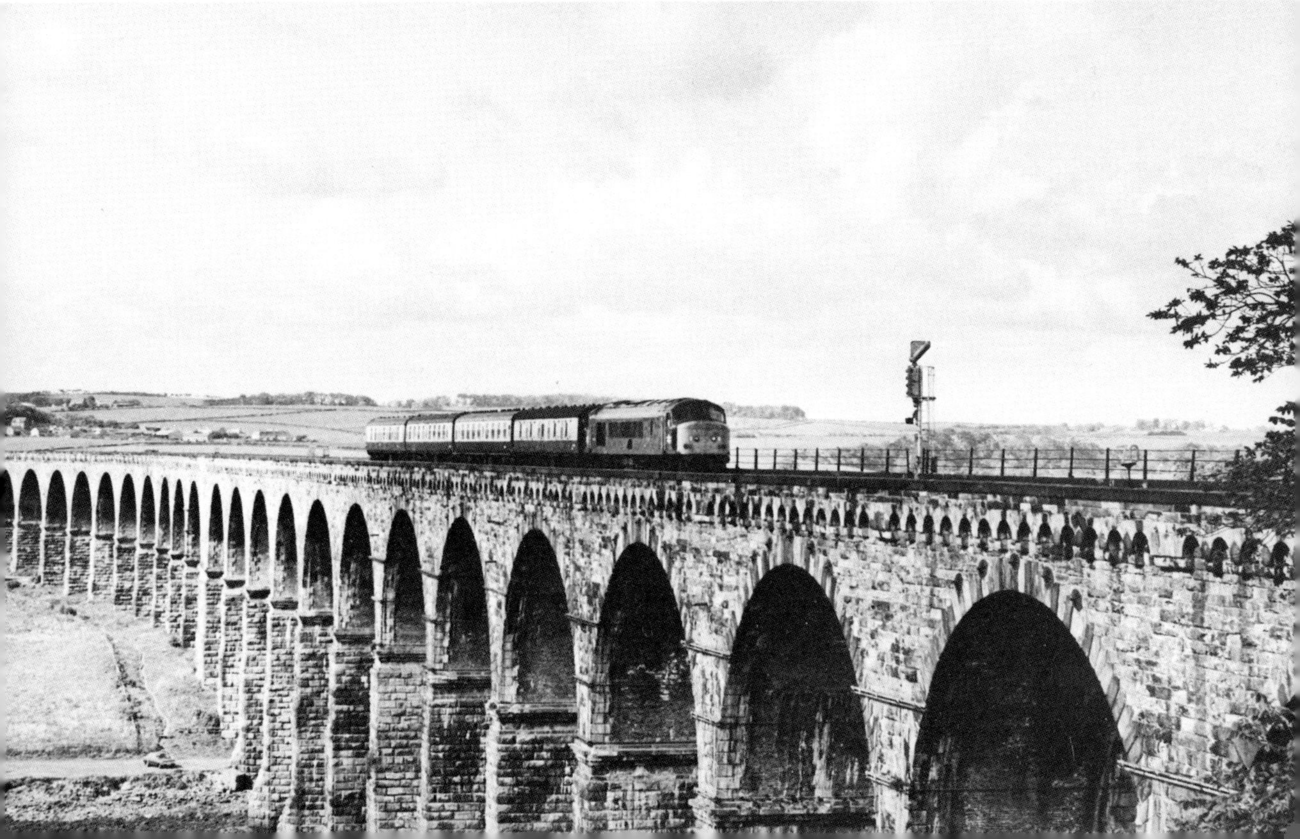